MAHATMA GANDHI

THE GREATEST INDIAN LAWYER

BABA MAHIR

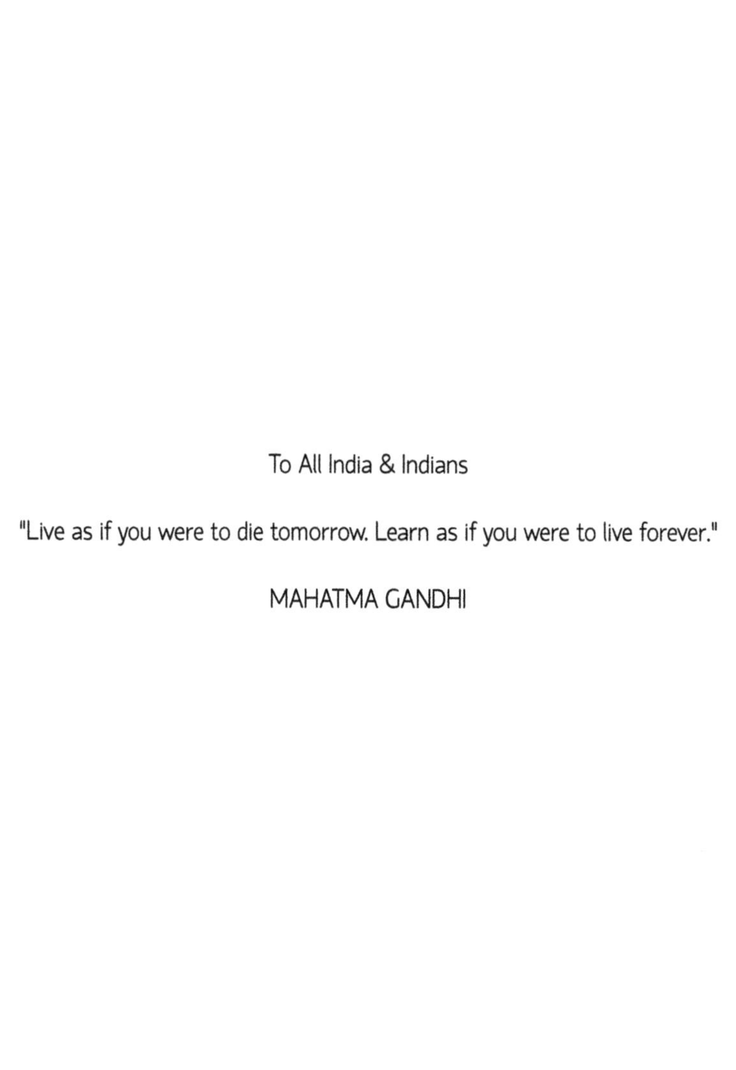

To All India & Indians

"Live as if you were to die tomorrow. Learn as if you were to live forever."

MAHATMA GANDHI

Contents

Foreword

Calling for non-violent civil disobedience, Gandhi led India to independence and inspired movements for civ. Though he studied law in London and spent his early adulthood in South Africa, he remained devoted to his homeland and spent the later part of his life working to make India an independent nation.

Revered the world over for his nonviolent philosophy of passive resistance, Mohandas Karamchand Gandhi was known to his many followers as Mahatma, or "the great-souled one." He began his activism as an Indian immigrant in South Africa in the early 1900s, and in the years following World War I became the leading figure

Preface

Mahatma Gandhi, byname of Mohandas Karamchand Gandhi, (born October 2, 1869, Porbandar, India—died January 30, 1948, Delhi), Indian lawyer, politician, social activist, and writer who became the leader of the nationalist movement against the British rule of Ind

"Live as if you were to die tomorrow. Learn as if you were to live forever." "Happiness is when what you think, what you say, and what you do are in harmony." "We may never be strong enough to be entirely nonviolent in thought, word and deed.

Acknowledgements

I wish to acknowledge with gratitude my indebtedness to all the persons and journals mentioned by me in connection with the anecdotes of Mahatma Gandhi narrated in this work.

A special debt of gratitude is due from me to the Notion Press Team. Especially Special Thankful to my Father (Nazir Ahmad). Love You Abu

BABA MAHIR

Prologue

The moment the mighty figure of Gandhi rises before us, the question presents itself: What is his relevance today and for the future? What inspiration can we draw from his life? What light can his thought and wisdom shed on our problems? How does his way of life affect our course of action in private and public affairs? That Gandhi is relevant today and for centuries to come is not in doubt at all. The words which Jawaharlal Nehru uttered almost immediately after Gandhi's sudden exit from this world are found to prove prophetic. He said, The light is gone and yet it will shine for a thousand years. Dr. Martin Luther King, Jr., the Nobel Peace Prize winner of U.S.A., came to India as a pilgrim in 1959. After a month's sojourn in the land of Gandhi, on the eve of his departure, he was asked a cynical question at a press conference in Delhi. Where is Gandhi today? He was asked: we see him nowhere. Dr. King's reply was that Gandhi was inevitable. If humanity is to progress, Gandhi is inescapable. He lived, thought and acted, inspired by the vision of a humanity evolving towards a world of peace and harmony. We may ignore him only at our own risk.

The relevance of a man or his message can be said to have many aspects. It can be immediate or remote; it can be local, regional or general; it can be personally relevant to some or universally for all. In the case of Gandhi all these aspects of his relevance can be studied with profit.

Man, in Gandhi's eyes, was the measure. Gandhi's approach to himself, and to life in general, was that of a seeker of truth and of a votary of nonviolence or love. His was a scientific mind and he sought for that law of life and being which would promote the common weal and help man to reach higher elevations of consciousness. He perceived that love, spelt as nonviolence in thought, word and deed, was the shortest cut to human progress and evolution, both individual and social. In his eyes, progressive nonviolence could express itself best through service, self-suffering and, if necessary, total sacrifice. His mind was always open, fresh and receptive to truth as he went on finding it from day to day by experience. For him, while his own consciousness was the laboratory for searching out the inner core of truth, human society was the field for social experiments which could lead to harmony and happiness. In whatever corner of the world he worked for the time being, the whole of humanity and its good were always present to him.

One very important aspect of his life adds measure significantly to what he thought and did. He lived day in and day out open to public view, as on a stage. He took the people and even his opponents into confidence not only in regard to his actions but even his motivations. The result is that none in history has left behind so much of documentation and direct evidence concerning everything he thought and did. Moreover, he himself has written so much and on every conceivable subject that his writings are likely to run into fifty to sixty sumptuous volumes of five hundred pages each. All this material is proving very helpful in assessing Gandhi's relevance both for the present and for the future.

It is impossible in a few brief pages to cover all the aspects of Gandhi's life and teaching which are of relevance to our own times and environment. Here I shall merely draw the attention of the reader to three aspects of his life which are of the utmost importance.

The life-story of Gandhi as a man is of the greatest relevance to every human being who aspires to rise above the average level and lead a meaningful life, with the watchword, "From good to better daily self-surpassed". Gandhi was not merely a moralist but one who believed that man has a great future and that he is evolving towards a higher and nobler destiny. He knew the power of the many vital and sensual urges of man. He has also confessed with remarkable frankness his own weaknesses in this matter. But what makes a study of his life most helpful is the unceasing attempt he makes to conquer these weaknesses and establish the superiority of moral and spiritual endeavour. Not one of us is free from the weaknesses our minds are subject to. At the same time, every one of us wishes to rise above the excessive demands of the flesh. This constant struggle goes on within us and we require not only inspiration and strength to win this inner battle but also some practical guidance to overcome our weaknesses. Gandhi is eminently fitted to be a good guide to us because he is extremely human and does not interpose any distance between himself and us by assuming an air of superiority or authority. He declared that what he had done, or was doing, every other human being was equally capable of doing. That self-control is the key to the higher and happier life was his constant refrain. His progress in this matter was not by a sudden conversion, or through the grace of some saint or seer or holy shrine. From and erring, faltering, stumbling and struggling youth, Gandhi rose to the eminence of being called "a moral genius" by no less a person than the celebrated British philosopher, C.E.M. Joad. This eminence he attained not be accident or luck or good fortune but by a determined and steady effort at self-discipline. His outer life and actions were but the reflection of his inner struggle to hold fast to truth, to truthful living, and to achiever good ends only through good, virtuous, nonviolent means. We can easily see what great importance he attached to self-control and personal virtue if we remember that he felt it necessary to take the vow of continence on the eve of launching the great campaign of satyagraha in South Africa. If one wishes to study a modern life, as in a film, a life which chastened itself from step to step and ultimately became the powerful force that raised a nation from utter slavery to dignified independence, one would have to go to Gandhi. There is something very intimate and personal, something very familiar and near in Gandhi's life because it is so open and sincere. Not only his celebrated autobiography, but his enormous and multitudinous correspondence and even the editorial columns of the journals which he edited for years and in which he always wrote in first person, all these reflect the process of his development from time to time. His every word, spoken or written, is like a link in the dialogue between his ego and his higher self.

It exposes to view the springs of motivation and action and thus renders the greatest service to man evolving from the stage of animality to humanity, from untruth to truth, from darkness to light, from hatred to love, from selfishness to altruism, from man the beast to man the god, which is really what all men aspire to be.

CHAPTER ONE

INTRODUCTION

Mahatma Gandhi, byname of Mohandas Karamchand Gandhi, (born October 2, 1869, Porbandar, India—died January 30, 1948, Delhi), Indian lawyer, politician, social activist, and writer who became the leader of the nationalist movement against the British rule of India. As such, he came to be considered the father of his country. Gandhi is internationally esteemed for his doctrine of nonviolent protest (satyagraha) to achieve political and social progress.

In the eyes of millions of his fellow Indians, Gandhi was the Mahatma ("Great Soul"). The unthinking adoration of the huge crowds that gathered to see him all along the route of his tours made them a severe ordeal; he could hardly work during the day or rest at night. "The woes of the Mahatmas," he wrote, "are known only to the Mahatmas." His fame spread worldwide during his lifetime and only increased after his death. The name Mahatma Gandhi is now one of the most universally recognized on earth.

The Development of Satyagraha

When he moved to South Africa in 1893, Gandhi quickly encountered racial discrimination. In a Durban court he was asked by the European magistrate to take off his turban; he refused and left the courtroom. A few days later, while traveling to Pretoria, he was thrown out of a first-class railway compartment and was later beaten up by the white driver of a stagecoach because he would not travel on the footboard to make room for a European passenger. He was also barred from hotels reserved "for Europeans only." But something happened to Gandhi as he smarted under the insults heaped upon him. That journey from Durban to Pretoria was his moment of truth. Henceforth he would not accept injustice. He would defend his dignity as an Indian and as a man. Gandhi fought with mixed success against South Africa's system of discrimination. He founded the Natal Indian Congress, and his writings exposed to the world the injustices suffered by Indians and others. In 1906 satyagraha ("devotion to truth") was born as a technique of nonviolent resistance. By the time Gandhi returned to India in 1915, he had developed satyagraha into an effective tool in the fight for social justice.

By 1920 Gandhi was India's dominant political figure, exerting a broad influence over the Indian population. The Indian National Congress (Congress Party) became a mass organization that Gandhi led in nonviolent actions. These included boycotts of British goods as well as British legislatures, courts, offices, and schools. In 1930 Gandhi launched the Salt March as a protest against a British tax on salt. The march was one of the most successful of Gandhi's campaigns. Yet by 1934 he had become disillusioned with the infighting among Congress Party members. He turned to building the nation "from the bottom up." By emphasizing rural education, social equality, and cottage industries, Gandhi believed India could become peaceful and self-sufficient. The final struggle for Indian independence began in 1942. Gandhi demanded an immediate British withdrawal from India, known as the Quit India Movement. Over the next five years Gandhi struggled to help Muslim, Hindu, and British leaders negotiate Indian independence. He was unable to block the Mountbatten Plan, which divided the subcontinent into a Hindu-majority India and Muslim-majority East and West Pakistan. On August 15, 1947, India achieved its independence. Gandhi worked to stop the Muslim-Hindu riots that followed. On January 30, 1948, he was assassinated by a Hindu radical who was upset by Gandhi's efforts to reconcile Hindus and Muslims.

Mahatma Gandhi is revered in India as the father of the country. He is remembered most for his nonviolent means of working for social justice, his acceptance of all faiths, and his ability to bring conflicting groups together. The model of satyagraha has inspired civil rights leaders, such as Martin Luther King, Jr., in many nations. Today Gandhi is one of the most universally known and revered figures in the world. In January 1997, nearly 50 years after his assassination, the ashes of Gandhi were spread in the Ganges River during a ceremony honoring his memory in Allahabad, India. The great-grandson of Gandhi, Tushar Gandhi, performed the act of dispersing the remains as thousands of onlookers chanted slogans in remembrance of the man who had succeeded, however briefly, in unifying a nation historically divided along religious and ethnic lines.

Initially, Gandhi's campaigns sought to combat the second-class status Indians received at the hands of the British regime. Eventually, however, they turned their focus to bucking the British regime altogether, a goal that was attained in the years directly after World War II. The victory was marred by the fact that sectarian violence within India between Hindus and Muslims necessitated the creation of two independent states—India and Pakistan—as opposed to a single unified India.

Gandhi's family practiced a kind of Vaishnavism, one of the major traditions within Hinduism, that was inflected through the morally rigorous tenets of Jainism—an Indian faith for which concepts like asceticism and nonviolence are important. Many of the beliefs that characterized Gandhi's spiritual outlook later in life may have originated in his upbringing. However, his understanding of faith was constantly evolving as he encountered new belief systems. Leo Tolstoy's analysis of Christian theology, for example, came to bear heavily on Gandhi's conception of spirituality, as did texts such as the Bible and the Qu'rān, and he first read the Bhagavadgita—a Hindu epic—in its English translation while living in Britain.

Within India, Gandhi's philosophy lived on in the messages of reformers such as social activist Vinoba Bhave. Abroad, activists such as Martin Luther King, Jr., borrowed heavily from Gandhi's practice of nonviolence and civil disobedience to achieve their own social equality aims. Perhaps most impactful of all, the freedom that Gandhi's movement won for India sounded a death knell for Britain's other colonial enterprises in Asia and Africa. Independence movements swept through them like wildfire, with Gandhi's influence bolstering existing movements and igniting new ones.

Gandhi's father was a local government official working under the suzerainty of the British Raj, and his mother was a religious devotee who—like the rest of the family—practiced in the Vaishnavist tradition of Hinduism. Gandhi married his wife, Kasturba, when he was 13, and together they had five children. His family stayed in India while Gandhi went to London in 1888 to study law and to South Africa in 1893 to practice it. He brought them to South Africa in 1897, where Kasturba would assist him in his activism, which she continued to do after the family moved back to India in 1915.

As lauded a figure as Gandhi has become, his actions and beliefs didn't escape the criticism of his contemporaries. Liberal politicians thought he was proposing too much change too quickly, while young radicals lambasted him for not proposing enough. Muslim leaders suspected him of lacking evenhandedness when dealing with Muslims and his own Hindu religious community, and Dalits (formerly called untouchables) thought him disingenuous in his apparent intention to abolish the caste system. He cut a controversial figure outside India as well, although for different reasons. The English—as India's colonizers—harboured some resentment toward him, as he toppled one of the first dominoes in their global imperial regime. But the image of Gandhi that has lasted is one that foregrounds his dogged fight against

CHAPTER TWO

YOUTH

Gandhi was the youngest child of his father's fourth wife. His father—Karamchand Gandhi, who was the dewan (chief minister) of Porbandar, the capital of a small principality in western India (in what is now Gujarat state) under British suzerainty—did not have much in the way of a formal education. He was, however, an able administrator who knew how to steer his way between the capricious princes, their long-suffering subjects, and the headstrong British political officers in power.

Gandhi's mother, Putlibai, was completely absorbed in religion, did not care much for finery or jewelry, divided her time between her home and the temple, fasted frequently, and wore herself out in days and nights of nursing whenever there was sickness in the family. Mohandas grew up in a home steeped in Vaishnavism—worship of the Hindu god Vishnu—with a strong tinge of Jainism, a morally rigorous Indian religion whose chief tenets are nonviolence and the belief that everything in the universe is eternal. Thus, he took for granted ahimsa (noninjury to all living beings), vegetarianism, fasting for self-purification, and mutual tolerance between adherents of various creeds and sects.

Get a Britannica Premium subscription and gain access to exclusive content.Subscribe Now

The educational facilities at Porbandar were rudimentary; in the primary school that Mohandas attended, the children wrote the alphabet in the dust with their fingers. Luckily for him, his father became dewan of Rajkot, another princely state. Though

Mohandas occasionally won prizes and scholarships at the local schools, his record was on the whole mediocre. One of the terminal reports rated him as "good at English, fair in Arithmetic and weak in Geography; conduct very good, bad handwriting." He was married at the age of 13 and thus lost a year at school. A diffident child, he shone neither in the classroom nor on the playing field. He loved to go out on long solitary walks when he was not nursing his by then ailing father (who died soon thereafter) or helping his mother with her household chores.

He had learned, in his words, "to carry out the orders of the elders, not to scan them." With such extreme passivity, it is not surprising that he should have gone through a phase of adolescent rebellion, marked by secret atheism, petty thefts, furtive smoking, and—most shocking of all for a boy born in a Vaishnava family—meat eating. His adolescence was probably no stormier than that of most children of his age and class. What was extraordinary was the way his youthful transgressions ended.

"Never again" was his promise to himself after each escapade. And he kept his promise. Beneath an unprepossessing exterior, he concealed a burning passion for self-improvement that led him to take even the heroes of Hindu mythology, such as Prahlada and Harishcandra—legendary embodiments of truthfulness and sacrifice—as living models.

In 1887 Mohandas scraped through the matriculation examination of the University of Bombay (now University of Mumbai) and joined Samaldas College in Bhavnagar (Bhaunagar). As he had to suddenly switch from his native language—Gujarati—to English, he found it rather difficult to follow the lectures.

Meanwhile, his family was debating his future. Left to himself, he would have liked to have been a doctor. But, besides the Vaishnava prejudice against vivisection, it was clear that, if he was to keep up the family tradition of holding high office in one of the states in Gujarat, he would have to qualify as a barrister. That meant a visit to England, and Mohandas, who was not too happy at

Samaldas College, jumped at the proposal. His youthful imagination conceived England as "a land of philosophers and poets, the very centre of civilization." But there were several hurdles to be crossed before the visit to England could be realized. His father had left the family little property; moreover, his mother was reluctant to expose her youngest child to unknown temptations and dangers in a distant land. But Mohandas was determined to visit England. One of his brothers raised the necessary money, and his mother's doubts were allayed when he took a vow that, while away from home, he would not touch wine, women, or meat. Mohandas disregarded the last obstacle—the decree of the leaders of the Modh Bania subcaste (Vaishya caste), to which the Gandhis belonged, who forbade his trip to England as a violation of the Hindu religion—and sailed in September 1888. Ten days after his arrival, he joined the Inner Temple, one of the four London law colleges (The Temple).

CHAPTER THREE

Sojourn in England and return to India of Mahatma Gandhi

Gandhi took his studies seriously and tried to brush up on his English and Latin by taking the University of London matriculation examination. But, during the three years he spent in England, his main preoccupation was with personal and moral issues rather than with academic ambitions. The transition from the half-rural atmosphere of Rajkot to the cosmopolitan life of London was not easy for him. As he struggled painfully to adapt himself to Western food, dress, and etiquette, he felt awkward. His vegetarianism became a continual source of embarrassment to him; his friends warned him that it would wreck his studies as well as his health. Fortunately for him he came across a vegetarian restaurant as well as a book providing a reasoned defense of vegetarianism, which henceforth became a matter of conviction for him, not merely a legacy of his Vaishnava background. The missionary zeal he developed for vegetarianism helped to draw the pitifully shy youth out of his shell and gave him a new poise. He became a member of the executive committee of the London Vegetarian Society, attending its conferences and contributing articles to its journal.

In the boardinghouses and vegetarian restaurants of England, Gandhi met not only food faddists but some earnest men and women to whom he owed his introduction to the Bible and, more important, the Bhagavadgita, which he read for the first time in its English translation by Sir Edwin Arnold. The Bhagavadgita (commonly known as the Gita) is part of the great epic the Mahabharata and, in the form of a philosophical poem, is the most-popular expression of Hinduism. The English vegetarians were a motley crowd. They included socialists and humanitarians such as Edward Carpenter, "the British Thoreau"; Fabians such as George Bernard Shaw; and Theosophists such as Annie Besant. Most of them were idealists; quite a few were rebels who rejected the prevailing values of the late-Victorian establishment, denounced the evils of the capitalist and industrial society, preached the cult of the simple life, and stressed the superiority of moral over material values and of cooperation over conflict. Those ideas were to contribute substantially to the shaping of Gandhi's personality and, eventually, to his politics.

Painful surprises were in store for Gandhi when he returned to India in July 1891. His mother had died in his absence, and he discovered to his dismay that the barrister's degree was not a guarantee of a lucrative career. The legal profession was already beginning to be overcrowded, and Gandhi was much too diffident to elbow his way into it. In the very first brief he argued in a court in Bombay (now Mumbai), he cut a sorry figure. Turned down even for the part-time job of a teacher in a Bombay high school, he returned to Rajkot to make a modest living by drafting petitions for litigants. Even that employment was closed to him when he incurred the displeasure of a local British officer. It was, therefore, with some relief that in 1893 he accepted the none-too-attractive offer of a year's contract from an Indian firm in Natal, South Africa.

CHAPTER FOUR

Years Of South Africa

Africa was to present to Gandhi challenges and opportunities that he could hardly have conceived. In the end he would spend more than two decades there, returning to India only briefly in 1896–97. The youngest two of his four children were born there.

Emergence as a political and social activist

Gandhi was quickly exposed to the racial discrimination practiced in South Africa. In a Durban court he was asked by the European magistrate to take off his turban; he refused and left the courtroom. A few days later, while traveling to Pretoria, he was unceremoniously thrown out of a first-class railway compartment and left shivering and brooding at the rail station in Pietermaritzburg. In the further course of that journey, he was beaten up by the white driver of a stagecoach because he would not travel on the footboard to make room for a European passenger, and finally he was barred from hotels reserved "for Europeans only." Those humiliations were the daily lot of Indian traders and labourers in Natal, who had learned to pocket them with the same resignation with which they pocketed their meagre earnings. What was new was not Gandhi's experience but his reaction. He had so far not been conspicuous for self-assertion or aggressiveness. But something happened to him as he smarted under the insults heaped upon him. In retrospect the journey from Durban to Pretoria struck him as one of the most-creative experiences of his life; it was his moment of truth. Henceforth he would not accept injustice as part of the natural or unnatural order in South Africa; he would defend his dignity as an Indian and as a man.

While in Pretoria, Gandhi studied the conditions in which his fellow South Asians in South Africa lived and tried to educate them on their rights and duties, but he had no intention of staying on in South Africa. Indeed, in June 1894, as his year's contract drew to a close, he was back in Durban, ready to sail for India. At a farewell party given in his honour, he happened to glance through the Natal Mercury and learned that the Natal Legislative Assembly was considering a bill to deprive Indians of the right to vote. "This is the first nail in our coffin," Gandhi told his hosts. They professed their inability to oppose the bill, and indeed their ignorance of the politics of the colony, and begged him to take up the fight on their behalf.

Until the age of 18, Gandhi had hardly ever read a newspaper. Neither as a student in England nor as a budding barrister in India had he evinced much interest in politics. Indeed, he was overcome by a terrifying stage fright whenever he stood up to read a speech at a social gathering or to defend a client in court. Nevertheless, in July 1894, when he was barely 25, he blossomed almost overnight into a proficient political campaigner. He drafted petitions to the Natal legislature and the British government and had them signed by hundreds of his compatriots. He could not prevent the passage of the bill but succeeded in drawing the attention of the public and the press in Natal, India, and England to the Natal Indians' grievances. He was persuaded to settle down in Durban to practice law and to organize the Indian community. In 1894 he founded the Natal Indian Congress, of which he himself became the indefatigable secretary. Through that common political organization, he infused a spirit of solidarity in the heterogeneous Indian community. He flooded the government, the legislature, and the press with closely reasoned statements of Indian grievances. Finally, he exposed to the view of the outside world the skeleton in the imperial cupboard, the discrimination practiced against the Indian subjects of Queen Victoria in one of her own colonies in Africa. It was a measure of his success as a publicist that such important newspapers as The Times of London and The Statesman and Englishman of Calcutta (now Kolkata) editorially commented on the Natal Indians' grievances.

In 1896 Gandhi went to India to fetch his wife, Kasturba (or Kasturbai), and their two oldest children and to canvass support for the Indians overseas. He met prominent leaders and persuaded them to address public meetings in the country's principal cities. Unfortunately for him, garbled versions of his activities and utterances reached Natal and inflamed its European population. On landing at Durban in January 1897, he was assaulted and nearly lynched by a white mob. Joseph Chamberlain, the colonial secretary in the British Cabinet, cabled the government of Natal to bring the guilty men to book, but Gandhi refused to prosecute his assailants. It was, he said, a principle with him not to seek redress of a personal wrong in a court of law.

CHAPTER FIVE

Resistance and results

Gandhi was not the man to nurse a grudge. On the outbreak of the South African (Boer) War in 1899, he argued that the Indians, who claimed the full rights of citizenship in the British crown colony of Natal, were in duty bound to defend it. He raised an ambulance corps of 1,100 volunteers, out of whom 300 were free Indians and the rest indentured labourers. It was a motley crowd: barristers and accountants, artisans and labourers. It was Gandhi's task to instill in them a spirit of service to those whom they regarded as their oppressors. The editor of the Pretoria News offered an insightful portrait of Gandhi in the battle zone:

After a night's work which had shattered men with much bigger frames, I came across Gandhi in the early morning sitting by the roadside eating a regulation army biscuit. Every man in [General] Buller's force was dull and depressed, and damnation was heartily invoked on everything. But Gandhi was stoical in his bearing, cheerful and confident in his conversation and had a kindly eye.

The British victory in the war brought little relief to the Indians in South Africa. The new regime in South Africa was to blossom into a partnership, but only between Boers and Britons. Gandhi saw that, with the exception of a few Christian missionaries and youthful idealists, he had been unable to make a perceptible impression upon the South African Europeans. In 1906 the Transvaal government published a particularly humiliating ordinance for the registration of its Indian population. The Indians held a mass protest meeting at Johannesburg in September 1906 and, under Gandhi's leadership, took a pledge to defy the ordinance if it became law in the teeth of their opposition and to suffer all the penalties resulting from their defiance. Thus was born satyagraha ("devotion to truth"), a new technique for redressing wrongs through inviting, rather than inflicting, suffering, for resisting adversaries without rancour and fighting them without violence.

What method of protest did Mohandas Gandhi advocate? Who was the first Sikh to serve as India's prime minister? Learn more about Gandhi and Indian history in this quiz.

The struggle in South Africa lasted for more than seven years. It had its ups and downs, but under Gandhi's leadership, the small Indian minority kept up its resistance against heavy odds. Hundreds of Indians chose to sacrifice their livelihood and liberty rather than submit to laws repugnant to their conscience and self-respect. In the final phase of the movement in 1913, hundreds of Indians, including women, went to jail, and thousands of Indian workers who had struck work in the mines bravely faced imprisonment, flogging, and even shooting. It was a terrible ordeal for the Indians, but it was also the worst possible advertisement for the South African government, which, under pressure from the governments of Britain and India, accepted a compromise negotiated by Gandhi on the one hand and the South African statesman Gen. Jan Christian Smuts on the other.

"The saint has left our shores," Smuts wrote to a friend on Gandhi's departure from South Africa for India, in July 1914, "I hope for ever." A quarter century later, he wrote that it had been his "fate to be the antagonist of a man for whom even then I had the highest respect." Once, during his not-infrequent stays in jail, Gandhi had prepared a pair of sandals for Smuts, who recalled that there was no hatred and personal ill-feeling between them, and when the fight was over "there was the atmosphere in which a decent peace could be concluded."

As later events were to show, Gandhi's work did not provide an enduring solution for the Indian problem in South Africa. What he did to South Africa was indeed less important than what South

Africa did to him. It had not treated him kindly, but, by drawing him into the vortex of its racial problem, it had provided him with the ideal setting in which his peculiar talents could unfold themselves.

CHAPTER SIX

The religious quest

Gandhi's religious quest dated back to his childhood, the influence of his mother and of his home life in Porbandar and Rajkot, but it received a great impetus after his arrival in South Africa. His Quaker friends in Pretoria failed to convert him to Christianity, but they quickened his appetite for religious studies. He was fascinated by the writings of Leo Tolstoy on Christianity, read the Qur'ān in translation, and delved into Hindu scriptures and philosophy. The study of comparative religion, talks with scholars, and his own reading of theological works brought him to the conclusion that all religions were true and yet every one of them was imperfect because they were "interpreted with poor intellects, sometimes with poor hearts, and more often misinterpreted."

Shrimad Rajchandra, a brilliant young Jain philosopher who became Gandhi's spiritual mentor, convinced him of "the subtlety and profundity" of Hinduism, the religion of his birth. And it was the Bhagavadgita, which Gandhi had first read in London, that became his "spiritual dictionary" and exercised probably the greatest single influence on his life. Two Sanskrit words in the Gita particularly fascinated him. One was aparigraha ("nonpossession"), which implies that people have to jettison the material goods that cramp the life of the spirit and to shake off the bonds of money and property. The other was samabhava ("equability"), which enjoins people to remain unruffled by pain or pleasure, victory or defeat, and to work without hope of success or fear of failure.

Those were not merely counsels of perfection. In the civil case that had taken him to South Africa in 1893, he had persuaded the antagonists to settle their differences out of court. The true function of a lawyer seemed to him "to unite parties riven asunder." He soon regarded his clients not as purchasers of his services but as friends; they consulted him not only on legal issues but on such matters as the best way of weaning a baby or balancing the family budget. When an associate protested that clients came even on Sundays, Gandhi replied: "A man in distress cannot have Sunday rest."

Gandhi's legal earnings reached a peak figure of £5,000 a year, but he had little interest in moneymaking, and his savings were often sunk in his public activities. In Durban and later in Johannesburg, he kept an open table; his house was a virtual hostel for younger colleagues and political coworkers. This was something of an ordeal for his wife, without whose extraordinary patience, endurance, and self-effacement Gandhi could hardly have devoted himself to public causes. As he broke through the conventional bonds of family and property, their life tended to shade into a community life.

Gandhi felt an irresistible attraction to a life of simplicity, manual labour, and austerity. In 1904—after reading John Ruskin's Unto This Last, a critique of capitalism—he set up a farm at Phoenix near Durban where he and his friends could live by the sweat of their brow. Six years later another colony grew up under Gandhi's fostering care near Johannesburg; it was named Tolstoy Farm for the Russian writer and moralist, whom Gandhi admired and corresponded with. Those two settlements were the precursors of the more-famous ashrams (religious retreats) in India, at Sabarmati near Ahmedabad (Ahmadabad) and at Sevagram near Wardha.

South Africa had not only prompted Gandhi to evolve a novel technique for political action but also transformed him into a leader of men by freeing him from bonds that make cowards of most men. "Persons in power," the British Classical scholar Gilbert Murray prophetically wrote about Gandhi in the Hibbert Journal in 1918, should be very careful how they deal with a man who cares nothing for sensual pleasure, nothing for riches, nothing for comfort or praise, or promotion, but is simply determined to do what he believes to be right. He is a dangerous and uncomfortable enemy, because his body which you can always conquer gives you so little purchase upon his soul.

CHAPTER SEVEN

Return to India

Gandhi decided to leave South Africa in the summer of 1914, just before the outbreak of World War I. He and his family first went to London, where they remained for several months. Finally, they departed England in December, arriving in Bombay in early January 1915.

Emergence as nationalist leader

For the next three years, Gandhi seemed to hover uncertainly on the periphery of Indian politics, declining to join any political agitation, supporting the British war effort, and even recruiting soldiers for the British Indian Army. At the same time, he did not flinch from criticizing the British officials for any acts of high-handedness or from taking up the grievances of the long-suffering peasantry in Bihar and Gujarat. By February 1919, however, the British had insisted on pushing through—in the teeth of fierce Indian opposition—the Rowlatt Acts, which empowered the authorities to imprison without trial those suspected of sedition. A provoked Gandhi finally revealed a sense of estrangement from the British raj and announced a satyagraha struggle. The result was a virtual political earthquake that shook the subcontinent in the spring of 1919. The violent outbreaks that followed—notably the Massacre of Amritsar, which was the killing by British-led soldiers of nearly 400 Indians who were gathered in an open space in Amritsar in the Punjab region (now in Punjab state), and the enactment of martial law—prompted him to stay his hand. However, within a year he was again in a militant mood, having in the meantime been irrevocably alienated by British insensitiveness to Indian feeling on the Punjab tragedy and Muslim resentment on the peace terms offered to Turkey following World War I.

By the autumn of 1920, Gandhi was the dominant figure on the political stage, commanding an influence never before attained by any political leader in India or perhaps in any other country. He refashioned the 35-year-old Indian National Congress (Congress Party) into an effective political instrument of Indian nationalism: from a three-day Christmas-week picnic of the upper middle class in one of the principal cities of India, it became a mass organization with its roots in small towns and villages. Gandhi's message was simple: it was not British guns but imperfections of Indians themselves that kept their country in bondage. His program, the nonviolent noncooperation movement against the British government, included boycotts not only of British manufactures but of institutions operated or aided by the British in India: legislatures, courts, offices, schools. The campaign electrified the country, broke the spell of fear of foreign rule, and led to the arrests of thousands of satyagrahis, who defied laws and cheerfully lined up for prison. In February 1922 the movement seemed to be on the crest of a rising wave, but, alarmed by a violent outbreak in Chauri Chaura, a remote village in eastern India, Gandhi decided to call off mass civil disobedience. That was a blow to many of his followers, who feared that his self-imposed restraints and scruples would reduce the nationalist struggle to pious futility. Gandhi himself was arrested on March 10, 1922, tried for sedition, and sentenced to six years' imprisonment. He was released in February 1924, after undergoing surgery for appendicitis. The political landscape had changed in his absence. The Congress Party had split into two factions, one under Chitta Ranjan Das and Motilal Nehru (the father of Jawaharlal Nehru, India's first prime minister) favouring the entry of the party into legislatures and the other under Chakravarti Rajagopalachari and Vallabhbhai Jhaverbhai Patel opposing it.

Worst of all, the unity between Hindus and Muslims of the heyday of the noncooperation movement of 1920–22 had dissolved. Gandhi tried to draw the warring communities out of their suspicion and fanaticism by reasoning and persuasion. Finally, after a serious outbreak of communal unrest, he undertook a three-week fast in the autumn of 1924 to arouse the people into following the path of nonviolence. In December 1924 he was named president of the Congress Party, and he served for a year.

CHAPTER EIGHT

Return to party leadership

During the mid-1920s Gandhi took little interest in active politics and was considered a spent force. In 1927, however, the British government appointed a constitutional reform commission under Sir John Simon, a prominent English lawyer and politician, that did not contain a single Indian. When the Congress and other parties boycotted the commission, the political tempo rose. At the Congress session (meeting) at Calcutta in December 1928, Gandhi put forth the crucial resolution demanding dominion status from the British government within a year under threat of a nationwide nonviolent campaign for complete independence. Henceforth, Gandhi was back as the leading voice of the Congress Party. In March 1930 he launched the Salt March, a satyagraha against the British-imposed tax on salt, which affected the poorest section of the community. One of the most spectacular and successful campaigns in Gandhi's nonviolent war against the British raj, it resulted in the imprisonment of more than 60,000 people. A year later, after talks with the viceroy, Lord Irwin (later Lord Halifax), Gandhi accepted a truce (the Gandhi-Irwin Pact), called off civil disobedience, and agreed to attend the Round Table Conference in London as the sole representative of the Indian National Congress.

Mohandas Gandhi and Sarojini Naidu

Mohandas Gandhi (left) and Sarojini Naidu (right) during the 1930 Salt March on the shore of Dandi, India.

Hulton Archive/Getty ImagesRound Table Conference

Mohandas K. Gandhi (front row, left) and other delegates attending the Round Table Conference in London, 1931.

Encyclopædia Britannica, Inc.

The conference, which concentrated on the problem of the Indian minorities rather than on the transfer of power from the British, was a great disappointment to the Indian nationalists. Moreover, when Gandhi returned to India in December 1931, he found his party facing an all-out offensive from Lord Irwin's successor as viceroy, Lord Willingdon, who unleashed the sternest repression in the history of the nationalist movement. Gandhi was once more imprisoned, and the government tried to insulate him from the outside world and to destroy his influence. That was not an easy task. Gandhi soon regained the initiative. In September 1932, while still a prisoner, he embarked on a fast to protest against the British government's decision to segregate the so-called "untouchables" (the lowest level of the Indian caste system; now called Scheduled Castes [official] or Dalits) by allotting them separate electorates in the new constitution. The fast produced an emotional upheaval in the country, and an alternative electoral arrangement was jointly and speedily devised by the leaders of the Hindu community and the Dalits and endorsed by the British government. The fast became the starting point of a vigorous campaign for the removal of the disenfranchisement of the Dalits, whom Gandhi referred to as Harijans, or "children of God."

In 1934 Gandhi resigned not only as the leader but also as a member of the Congress Party. He had come to believe that its leading members had adopted nonviolence as a political expedient and not as the fundamental creed it was for him. In place of political activity he then concentrated on his "constructive programme" of building the nation "from the bottom up"—educating rural India, which accounted for 85 percent of the population; continuing his fight against untouchability; promoting hand spinning, weaving, and other cottage industries to supplement the earnings of the underemployed peasantry; and evolving a system of education best suited to the needs of the people. Gandhi himself went to live at

Sevagram, a village in central India, which became the centre of his program of social and economic uplift.

CHAPTER NINE

The last phase

With the outbreak of World War II, the nationalist struggle in India entered its last crucial phase. Gandhi hated fascism and all it stood for, but he also hated war. The Indian National Congress, on the other hand, was not committed to pacifism and was prepared to support the British war effort if Indian self-government was assured. Once more Gandhi became politically active. The failure of the mission of Sir Stafford Cripps, a British cabinet minister who went to India in March 1942 with an offer that Gandhi found unacceptable, the British equivocation on the transfer of power to Indian hands, and the encouragement given by high British officials to conservative and communal forces promoting discord between Muslims and Hindus impelled Gandhi to demand in the summer of 1942 an immediate British withdrawal from India—what became known as the Quit India Movement.

In mid-1942 the war against the Axis powers, particularly Japan, was in a critical phase, and the British reacted sharply to the campaign. They imprisoned the entire Congress leadership and set out to crush the party once and for all. There were violent outbreaks that were sternly suppressed, and the gulf between Britain and India became wider than ever before. Gandhi, his wife, and several other top party leaders (including Nehru) were confined in the Aga Khan Palace (now the Gandhi National Memorial) in Poona (now Pune). Kasturba died there in early 1944, shortly before Gandhi and the others were released.

A new chapter in Indo-British relations opened with the victory of the Labour Party in Britain 1945. During the next two years, there were prolonged triangular negotiations between leaders of the Congress, the Muslim League under Mohammed Ali Jinnah, and the British government, culminating in the Mountbatten Plan of June 3, 1947, and the formation of the two new dominions of India and Pakistan in mid-August 1947.

Funeral procession for Mohandas (Mahatma) Gandhi, February 2, 1948, with a quote from the eulogy by Prime Minister Jawaharlal Nehr

It was one of the greatest disappointments of Gandhi's life that Indian freedom was realized without Indian unity. Muslim separatism had received a great boost while Gandhi and his colleagues were in jail, and in 1946–47, as the final constitutional arrangements were being negotiated, the outbreak of communal riots between Hindus and Muslims unhappily created a climate in which Gandhi's appeals to reason and justice, tolerance and trust had little chance. When partition of the subcontinent was accepted—against his advice—he threw himself heart and soul into the task of healing the scars of the communal conflict, toured the riot-torn areas in Bengal and Bihar, admonished the bigots, consoled the victims, and tried to rehabilitate the refugees. In the atmosphere of that period, surcharged with suspicion and hatred, that was a difficult and heartbreaking task. Gandhi was blamed by partisans of both the communities. When persuasion failed, he went on a fast. He won at least two spectacular triumphs: in September 1947 his fasting stopped the rioting in Calcutta, and in January 1948 he shamed the city of Delhi into a communal truce. A few days later, on January 30, while he was on his way to his evening prayer meeting in Delhi, he was shot down by Nathuram Godse, a young Hindu fanatic.

CHAPTER TEN

Place in history of Mahatma Gandhi

The British attitude toward Gandhi was one of mingled admiration, amusement, bewilderment, suspicion, and resentment. Except for a tiny minority of Christian missionaries and radical socialists, the British tended to see him at best as a utopian visionary and at worst as a cunning hypocrite whose professions of friendship for the British race were a mask for subversion of the British raj. Gandhi was conscious of the existence of that wall of prejudice, and it was part of the strategy of satyagraha to penetrate it.

His three major campaigns in 1920–22, 1930–34, and 1940–42 were well designed to engender that process of self-doubt and questioning that was to undermine the moral defenses of his adversaries and to contribute, together with the objective realities of the postwar world, to producing the grant of dominion status in 1947. The British abdication in India was the first step in the liquidation of the British Empire on the continents of Asia and Africa. Gandhi's image as a rebel and enemy died hard, but, as it had done to the memory of George Washington, Britain, in 1969, the centenary year of Gandhi's birth, erected a statue to his memory.

Gandhi had critics in his own country and indeed in his own party. The liberal leaders protested that he was going too fast; the young radicals complained that he was not going fast enough; left-wing politicians alleged that he was not serious about evicting the British or liquidating such vested Indian interests as princes and landlords; the leaders of the Dalits doubted his good faith as a social reformer; and Muslim leaders accused him of partiality to his own community.

Research in the second half of the 20th century established Gandhi's role as a great mediator and reconciler. His talents in that direction were applied to conflicts between the older moderate politicians and the young radicals, the political terrorists and the parliamentarians, the urban intelligentsia and the rural masses, the traditionalists and the modernists, the caste Hindus and the Dalits, the Hindus and the Muslims, and the Indians and the British.

It was inevitable that Gandhi's role as a political leader should loom larger in the public imagination, but the mainspring of his life lay in religion, not in politics. And religion for him did not mean formalism, dogma, ritual, or sectarianism. "What I have been striving and pining to achieve these thirty years," he wrote in his autobiography, "is to see God face to face." His deepest strivings were spiritual, but unlike many of his fellow Indians with such aspirations, he did not retire to a cave in the Himalayas to meditate on the Absolute; he carried his cave, as he once said, within him. For him truth was not something to be discovered in the privacy of one's personal life; it had to be upheld in the challenging contexts of social and political life.

Gandhi won the affection and loyalty of gifted men and women, old and young, with vastly dissimilar talents and temperaments; of Europeans of every religious persuasion; and of Indians of almost every political line. Few of his political colleagues went all the way with him and accepted nonviolence as a creed; fewer still shared his food fads, his interest in mudpacks and nature cure, or his prescription of brahmacarya, complete renunciation of the pleasures of the flesh.

Gandhi's ideas on sex may now sound quaint and unscientific. His marriage at the age of 13 seems to have complicated his attitude toward sex and charged it with feelings of guilt, but it is important to remember that total sublimation, according to one tradition of Hindu thought, is indispensable for those who seek self-realization, and brahmacarya was for Gandhi part of a larger discipline in food, sleep, thought, prayer, and daily activity designed to equip himself for service of the causes to which he was totally committed. What he failed to see was that his own unique experience was no guide for the common man.

Scholars have continued to judge Gandhi's place in history. He was the catalyst if not the initiator of three of the major revolutions of the 20th century: the movements against colonialism, racism, and violence. He wrote copiously; the collected edition of his writings had reached 100 volumes by the early 21st century.

Much of what he wrote was in response to the needs of his coworkers and disciples and the exigencies of the political situation, but on fundamentals he maintained a remarkable consistency, as is evident from the Hind Swaraj ("Indian Home Rule"), published in South Africa in 1909. The strictures on Western materialism and colonialism, the reservations about industrialism and urbanization, the distrust of the modern state, and the total rejection of violence that was expressed in that book seemed romantic, if not reactionary, to the pre-World War I generation in India and the West, which had not known the shocks of two global wars or experienced the phenomenon of Adolf Hitler and the trauma of the atom bomb. Prime Minister Jawaharlal Nehru's objective of promoting a just and egalitarian order at home and nonalignment with military blocs abroad doubtless owed much to Gandhi, but neither he nor his colleagues in the Indian nationalist movement wholly accepted the Gandhian models in politics and economics.

In the years since Gandhi's death, his name has been invoked by the organizers of numerous demonstrations and movements. However, with a few outstanding exceptions—such as those of his disciple the land reformer Vinoba Bhave in India and of the civil rights leader Martin Luther King, Jr., in the United States—those movements have been a travesty of the ideas of Gandhi.

Yet Gandhi will probably never lack champions. Erik H. Erikson, a distinguished American psychoanalyst, in his study of Gandhi senses "an affinity between Gandhi's truth and the insights of modern psychology." One of the greatest admirers of Gandhi was Albert Einstein, who saw in Gandhi's nonviolence a possible antidote to the massive violence unleashed by the fission of the atom. And Gunnar Myrdal, the Swedish economist, after his survey of the socioeconomic problems of the underdeveloped world, pronounced Gandhi "in practically all fields an enlightened liberal." In a time of deepening crisis in the underdeveloped world, of social malaise in the affluent societies, of the shadow of unbridled technology and the precarious peace of nuclear terror, it seems likely that Gandhi's ideas and techniques will become increasingly relevant.

Summary

Mahatma Gandhi, byname of Mohandas Karamchand Gandhi, (born Oct. 2, 1869, Porbandar, India—died Jan. 30, 1948, Delhi), Preeminent leader of Indian nationalism and prophet of nonviolence in the 20th century.

Gandhi grew up in a home steeped in religion, and he took for granted religious tolerance and the doctrine of ahimsa (noninjury to all living beings). He studied law in England from 1888 to 1891, and in 1893 he took a job with an Indian firm in South Africa. There he became an effective advocate for Indian rights.

In 1906 he first put into action satyagraha, his technique of nonviolent resistance. His success in South Africa gave him an international reputation, and in 1915 he returned to India and within a few years became the leader of a nationwide struggle for Indian home rule. By 1920 Gandhi commanded influence hitherto unattained by any political leader in India.

He refashioned the Indian National Congress into an effective political instrument of Indian nationalism and undertook major campaigns of nonviolent resistance in 1920–22, 1930–34 (including his momentous march to the sea to collect salt to protest a government monopoly), and 1940–42. In the 1930s he also campaigned to end discrimination against India's lower-caste "untouchables" (Dalits; officially designated as Scheduled Castes) and concentrated on educating rural India and promoting cottage industry.

India achieved dominion status in 1947, but the partition of the subcontinent into India and Pakistan was a great disappointment to Gandhi, who had long worked for Hindu-Muslim unity. In September 1947 he ended rioting in Calcutta (Kolkata) by fasting. Known as the Mahatma ("Great-Souled"), Gandhi had won the affection and loyalty of millions. In January 1948 he was shot and killed by a young Hindu fanatic.

Timeline

Mahatma Gandhi was one of the greatest national and civil rights leaders of the 20th century. He served as a lawyer, politician, and activist in the struggle for social justice and for India's independence from British rule. Gandhi is internationally esteemed for his doctrine of nonviolent protest (satyagraha) to achieve political and social progress.

Printed by Libri Plureos GmbH in Hamburg,
Germany